D1125359

Gandhi's Seven Steps
to Global Change

Gandhi's

Seven Steps to

Global Change

by Guy de Mallac

A Peacewatch Edition

Ocean Tree Books • Santa Fe

Published by:

Ocean Tree Books
Post Office Box 1295
Santa Fe, New Mexico 87504 U.S.A.

If you wish to communicate with the author, Guy de Mallac, and explore the Gandhian message further, please write:

Center for Nonviolence & Voluntary Service
Post Office Box 1058
San Jacinto, California 92383 U.S.A.

Designed by Richard Polese
Typeset by David Delugach

ISBN: 0-943734-16-9

Library of Congress C.I.P. data:

```
Mallac, Guy de, 1936-
    Gandhi's seven steps to global change / by Guy de Mallac.
    1. Gandhi, Mahatma, 1869-1948--Political and social views.
2. World politics--1985-1995.  3. Economic history--1971-
I. Mallac, Guy de, 1936-  Gandhi's message for today.  II. Title.
III. Series. (A Peacewatch edition)
DS481.G3M279  1989                                      90-6883
954.03'5'092--dc20                                      CIP
```

CONTENTS

THE GANDHIAN PROGRAM FOR GLOBAL CONVERSION

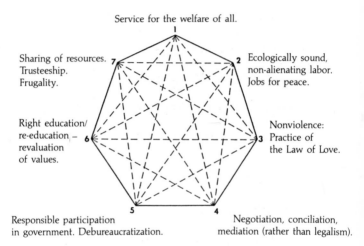

Service for the welfare of all.

Sharing of resources.
Trusteeship.
Frugality.

Ecologically sound,
non-alienating labor.
Jobs for peace.

Right education/
re-education –
revaluation
of values.

Nonviolence:
Practice of
the Law of Love.

Responsible participation
in government. Debureaucratization.

Negotiation, conciliation,
mediation (rather than legalism).

(Achieving one goal fosters the achievement of each of the other goals or points in the program.
Non-achievement of any one goal is a potential hindrance to the achievement of the other goals.)

INTRODUCTION

The Gandhi Challenge

Today's world is in the throes of several global crises that have repercussions for us all. One billion human beings are functioning on an average income of less than $200 a year — malnutrition and starvation are taking their toll on those living on such meager resources. Swelled by growing numbers of underprivileged people who seek subsistence from day to day, world population, now at five billion, is on its way to reaching six billion by the year 2000.

Precious nonrenewable energy resources are being squandered, while we are witnessing a runaway deterioration and loss of resources essential for agriculture. All the while, we are living in the shadow and insecurity of a formidable escalation in the production of lethal weapons — a colossal waste of the world's resources, amounting to an annual world-wide consumption of $660 billion that could be used to alleviate the basic needs of humanity.

What can Gandhi's message contribute toward the solving of these momentous problems? Simply said, his message brings *crucially relevant solutions*.

Mohandas Karamchand Gandhi (1869-1948) was known to hundreds of millions of Indians and Westerners as the "Mahatma" or "great Soul" whose skillful strategy of nonviolence, combined with a simple human vision, brought about the emancipation of India in the 1940s. He was the most decisive theoretician and the most spectacular practitioner of nonviolence — a doctrine which meshed closely with specific points of his global program of social reform.

Gandhi's most prominent disciple was the Rev. Martin Luther King, Jr. (1929-1968), a principal leader and theoretician in the nonviolent civil rights movement in the United States.

Beginning with his leadership in the Montgomery bus boycott in 1955, through eleven years of intensive civil rights action, King inspired and organized an explicitly nonviolent mass movement to challenge racial discrimination. Through his campaigns, he took the lead in exercising and extending civil rights (and with them, personal pride and dignity) that had been denied to black Americans since their arrival on this continent. Like Gandhi, King was assassinated because of his efforts to end discrimination among ethnic and cultural groups.

The aim of this booklet is to make clear the relevance of Gandhi's and King's strategy to today's world. For most contemporary issues, Gandhi and King came up with very specific strategies and guildelines; for the rest, it is clear which strategies should be pursued within the spirit of the Gandhian message.

We will examine seven general problems in the world, with corresponding Gandhian solutions. These seven solutions are closely related to one another. Gandhi's overall strategy for peace and justice hinged upon the practice of all seven solutions: selfless service, fair and right labor, love and nonviolence, conciliation, participation in government, education/re-education, and sharing of resources. These points of his integrated *constructive program* (as he termed it) reinforce one another. Together, they constitute a complete, encompassing (some might say "holistic") philosophy of life and action.

The Gandhian strategy is a challenge to us. If we want a world that is secure and human, we have a responsibility to change our lives! We have a responsibility to make changes around us that will improve the lives of others. Each section of this little book suggests involvement in action that will make a difference around us. The appendix gives concrete hints and recommendations about specific forms of action.

Gandhi's Seven Steps
to Global Change

1
SELFLESS SERVICE FOR THE WELFARE OF ALL

> *Problem:*
>
> Unrestrained **selfishness** creates havoc. We often seek self-promotion regardless of how much it may hurt others.

Gandhi's strategy of nonviolence is intimately related to his overall world view (which is based upon his close acquaintance with the major religious traditions). That world view boils down to four very simple, interrelated principles:

1. In spite of the seeming or real diversity and complexity of the forms of life, there is the unity of all life. Such unity exists, insofar as all forms of life participate in the same overall cosmic reality. We are all intimately interrelated. We are all members of the same family, like cells of the same organism. Therefore, strictly speaking, it is not possible for me to hurt and damage someone else without hurting and damaging myself. Sooner or later, in however unexpected a form, the hurt we cause to others catches up with us. This truth is fundamental to Christianity, Buddhism, and other religions.

   There are various contemporary corroborations of that Gandhian perception. Thus, modern science allows us to perceive more clearly than ever before the unity and interconnectedness of all life, and the fact that all life is completely interdependent; that Earth is one gigantic organism — a "single, fragile life support system." Most fortunately, the Beyond War movement is currently stressing this point. It says that a narrow identification (with our body, our family, clan, nation, or race) leads to an illusion of separateness and division. However, we have an alternative to such narrow identification: expanded identification allows us to identify with the whole, with all of humanity.

2. There is a superior cosmic reality, whose voice Gandhi feels is the individual's *conscience* — the "still small voice" within each of us that lets us know what is truthful and what is not. Of course, there are many ways whereby we can reject or block out this voice of conscience. But even when other forms of religious experience or practice are not available, even if there are no special intermediaries such as pastors, ritual, or scripture, the basic way this great cosmic being has of speaking to us is through conscience, from inside. Perhaps conscience is another term for our ability to do away with self-deception, and confront a demanding Truth.

3. The religious message we receive through our conscience is *universal*. That message is the common denominator of the highest religious and moral-philosophical doctrines. No one can claim to be outside the jurisdiction of that message. Its appeal is universal because it is inscribed in the hearts of all women and men in all cultural and religious contexts.

4. That supreme cosmic reality makes itself known to us through conscience. In the social realm it becomes an appeal *to serve*. What Gandhi is talking about is selfless service, the kind which flowed from the dedicated lives of persons such as Albert Schweitzer, Mother Teresa, and Gandhi himself. Without denying that there is scope for

the unique development of the individual who is engaged in serving others, he feels such service is "selfless" in that it teaches us to transcend the finite, limited ego. Gandhi comes up with very stark formulas, almost too stark and abrasive for most of us, about what that service means. According to him, religion or service consists in giving ourselves to the most destitute around us: "Religion is service to the helpless." This disturbing statement may leave some of us out in the cold, just when we were feeling we were nicely religious individuals. Religion, in this Gandhian sense, in this purified and refined sense that he and his teacher, the writer and sage Leo Tolstoy[1], believe in, means selfless commitment.

Closer to us, two exponents of the Gandhian tradition have conveyed the same message. Martin Luther King, Jr., said, "The true neighbor will risk his position, his prestige, and even his life for the welfare of others." And more recently, Cesar Chavez gave us a lesson in courageous sacrifice when he asserted: "To be a man is to suffer for others."

> *The poor, the illiterate, the ignorant, the afflicted — let these be your God. Know that service to these alone is the highest religion.*
>
> — *Swami Vivekananda*

---

1. Gandhi referred to Tolstoy as his "guru" or teacher — insofar as some of Tolstoy's social-philosophical writings triggered Gandhi's conversion to the strategy of nonviolence.

Solution:

Work for **the welfare of all people.** Practice the Golden Rule. Love all humans as brothers and sisters. Since life includes respect, we must promote universal acceptance and universal sisterhood/brotherhood/ familyhood. **Challenge all discriminations and prejudices.** Withdraw support from repressive and oppressive policies at home or abroad. Promote the dignity of human beings regardless of age, sex, race, or creed.

Service is service to your neighbor. . . Your neighbor is the symbol of society. . . Your neighbor is the most difficult being in the world to love. . . Every person who needs your help, however far he or she may be on this globe, is your neighbor.

— An Indian disciple of Gandhi

2
RIGHT AND FAIR LABOR

Problem:

The weak, the poor, and the disenfranchised are crushed under the weight of **harsh living and working conditions**. In areas where human labor is plentiful, there is a scarcity or unavailability of work, as a result of development which is technology intensive. Work opportunities are concentrated in urban centers where conditions are harsher for the poor; available jobs are not fulfilling. Large, technology centered, urban / industrial centers are impersonal and alienating. **"Big" is impersonal and alienating**.

In the Gandhian tradition, our work is the most crucial practical opportunity we have to apply our desire to bring about greater peace and social justice. (Using Gandhian terminology, we could say, "Our work is our prayer.") How we invest our talents and energies can potentially foster peace and justice around us. For example, so long as through our work we continue to take advantage of those who are economically weaker, there will be injustice; peace will be jeopardized. The place to start, the first concrete step we should all try to take, is to practice the right kind of work.

Gandhi's mentor Tolstoy came to the conclusion that choosing to practice an occupation that merely "amuses the well-fed" weighs very, very low on the moral scale. For those of us who have a choice (and many of the underprivileged do not), practicing the kind of work that merely aims at titillating the overjaded senses and tastes of those who are already overprivileged receives a low rating in the Gandhian perspective.

Whereas efforts to help the masses solve their plight receive a high rating on the Gandhian scale. Morally speaking, our vocations and avocations rate very high if they help improve the quality of life for those sixty to eighty percent of humankind who are underprivileged, and rate very low if they worsen their situation. The ideal is for us to make the essence of our occupation something that will help solve the plight of the downtrodden, by supplying them with basic necessities — food, shelter, and especially a chance to work. Instead of devoting our best efforts to "lightening and embellishing the idleness" of the overprivileged few, we should seek through our occupation to improve the lives of the many human beings who are crushed by exhaustion, hunger, and unpalatable or oppressive labor.

In the Gandhian tradition, work which helps to attain this goal is characterized as "bread-labor," i.e., "all the heavy, rough work necessary to save humans from death by hunger and cold." For Gandhi, bread-labor is several things simultaneously: a kind of minimum physical labor which must be performed by everybody, from the philosopher to the ordinary laborers; labor for the purpose of earning a living; an instrument of self-actualization; and a method of service to others.

According to the Gandhian view, anyone who tries to escape heavy, rough work in order to practice a more easygoing occupation is partaking of the unbalance which crushes the weak with overwork while the economically strong are freed from the less desirable forms of "rough work." While completely forsaking an easygoing job in order to practice some less desirable form of rough work may be an unrealistic goal for many, there are a number of possible intermediate solutions — such as devoting only five or ten percent of our time to a "less desirable" form of work that will allow us to commune with the vast majority of the underprivileged. Far from being a token gesture, any step in that direction concretely helps to correct the unbalance. Because it promotes equality between the classes and compassion for the poor, that Gandhian doctrine of bread-labor "has the potential to affect a silent revolution in the structure of society." (J.D. Sethi)

In fostering authenticity through work, Gandhi recommends the practice of an appropriate and suitably balanced reliance on machinery and technology — alongside the practice of handcrafts. In spite of a misconception which some have perpetuated, Gandhi did not reject technology and industrialization in themselves. He was all in favor of industrialization, so long as technology and mass production techniques do not take over and work against humankind's best interests (this they do when they are "labor saving" to the extent of dispensing with the labor of millions of human beings and putting them out of work).

Within the Gandhian tradition, British economist E.F. Schumacher has given us an outline of Gandhian economics in his book, *Small is Beautiful: Economics as if People Mattered.* Schumacher speaks up on behalf of the emerging post-industrial society, one "that has left behind its lethal obsession with megasystems of production and distribution." He stresses that what we really require from science and technology are methods and equipment which are cheap enough so that they are accessible to virtually everyone, suitable for small-scale application, and compatible with the human need for creativity. (Ideally, this need for creativity in our work is usually better fulfilled through meaningful interaction with a limited number of individuals — as opposed to a large, anonymous mass.) Schumacher's concern for an economic approach centered on regionalism is echoed by Kirkpatrick Sale in his recent and immensely stimulating book, *Dwellers in the Land: The Bioregional Vision.*

Because of its insistence that the right approach to labor is essential to an integrated strategy for peace, Gandhian practice has long fostered the spirit underlying today's blueprints for Peace Conversion Economics — the process by which industries are converted from military research and production to civilian manufacturing of consumer goods.

Today we are faced with a crying need to foster such a process. Since World War II the United States has maintained a permanent war economy; our military spending now surpasses that at the height of that war, in 1945. The knowledge and skills presently being drained off by research and manufacture of war material could be utilized in civilian pursuits and in production of consumer goods essential for a healthy economy. Incessant production of war material is inflationary because it puts money into circulation without a concomitant supply of consumer goods. Workers in the so-called "defense" industry, in particular, must be made to see that their ultimate job security depends on early and comprehensive peace conversion planning. Many more jobs per dollar spent are realized in a civilian economy than in war production; when awareness of this fact grows, there will be a greater motivation to facilitate the transition from a war to a peace economy. The peace conversion planning process must involve workers, management, the community, and local and state government. According to the analysis of the California-based Center for Economic Conversion, there are four elements in such a process: advance planning before dislocations occur; participation of the workforce, management, and the community; optimum use of existing capacity; and production of socially needed goods and services.

This challenge of the conversion of our economy to peaceful purposes has to be met — or else, through the very nature of much of the labor that supports it, our society will continue fostering the current upward spiraling of violence that can only lead to disaster.

> *Love for humankind won't let us serve it by (making our work consist of) amusing the well-fed, while leaving the cold and hungry to die of want.*
>
> — *Tolstoy*

> *Gandhian bread-labor has the potential to effect a silent revolution in the structure of society.*
>
> — *Economist J.D. Sethi*

Solution:

Foster the right approach to work. Give **the right to work** to all human beings. Promote self-help, autonomy, and self-sufficiency. Support **cooperative** approaches to work and economic problems. Practice right ecology and appropriate/intermediate technology. **Small is beautiful** — small preserves a human scale and more human relationships.

3
LOVE AND NONVIOLENCE

Problem:

In a violent conflict, the **law of aggression** is allowed to take over. We become resigned to war as a "necessary evil." Nuclearism is the ultimate violence.

We have examined Gandhi's thoughts on selfless service. We have surveyed his ideas relating to frugality and simplicity. We have analyzed his concepts about work. All of these relate to his nonviolent approach to life. Now let us look at nonviolence itself, directly.

To understand it clearly, we have to focus once again on Gandhi's overall world view. We have to grasp the initial essential fact: a fundamental basic unity exists between us all. We are all members of the same body.

If we are all members of the same family, part of the same reality, we should understand that truth is also in *others*, not just in ourselves alone. Truth is also in our adversary. The adversary's truth may be a truth — or a relative truth — for him or her, if not for me; and I should respect his or her right to be guided by it. We find notations to that effect in major scripture and philosophical statements in all civilizations. "If we drop our narrow frame of reference, and give credence to what others have experienced, we come closer to understanding the true nature of our world."

This concept should help us overcome the undue sense of righteousness and inner morality that makes us see others as entrenched enemies who are not partaking of our limited truth. We can grow by seeing others as part of our same reality; we can learn from them, respect them, and relate lovingly to them — even when we do not fully approve of their principles or behavior.

In some cases, only a very thin layer of truth, or of a semblance of truth, may be left in an individual — along with considerable untruth, and violent and evil behavior. But we should always allow at least the theoretical possibility that the opponent may see the light, or be affected by an inner light. Besides, as Martin Luther King firmly believed, nonviolence should be directed "against forces of evil rather than against the persons who committed the evil." The opponent is merely the symbol of a greater evil — and thus (as William Watley stated in a recent study) King "depersonalized the target of the nonviolent resister's attack." King viewed opponents as "human beings . . . to be respected and not violated."

Gandhi used an explanation that he borrowed from Tolstoy, claiming that there are two principles at work within us. We are a battleground between these two principles. One he called the *Law of Love*; the other, the *Law of Violence* or Aggression. Gandhi acknowledges that both exist. The Law of Love is a force which is present and deeply seated and felt in all of us. It exists inside us; it is something within others that we can reach out toward. Even in the case of the most hardened criminal there is still, theoretically, always a possibility to reach out to that place. And we may be certain that in each individual there is a readiness to respond when reached out to.

The Law of Violence or Aggression is also present in us. Gandhi certainly did not deny it. It exists in human activities. It exists in the animal kingdom. We should beware, however, of those negative thinkers who tell us that "there always has been war and there always will be." Strife and war, such persons say, are fine and good things for humans. In certain traditions, such as the militaristic circles in Bismarckian Germany, the notion existed that war was a wholesome hygiene that allowed human nature to be perked up when civilization was becoming too soft. According to that world view (still prevalent in certain quarters), aggression is healthier than non-aggression, waging war is an invigorating activity, and it is totally positive to behave aggressively. This is not Gandhi's perspective.

We very often, and mistakenly, ascribe this attitude of aggression to the animal world. This is reflected by our language in such statements as "dog eats dog" or "man is a wolf to man." However, this is not so. All those who have taken the time to study the behavior of wild beasts tell us that only in the rarest of instances will wolf eat fellow wolf. But alas, it seems to be a peculiarity of *our* species that we should go out and annihilate others of the same species, sometimes in the most systematic and horrendous ways. We have to be clear that this is not something we can just ascribe to our animal heritage.

We should be aware, however, that there is a tendency in human nature to exert pressure, and undue pressure, on others. Aggression and aggressiveness can take different forms. Social and economic oppression, whereby the poor are left with society's dirty work, is but one example. However, we should also be aware that there is inscribed in us that other force, the Law of Love, the practice of which will help neutralize or tone down raw aggressiveness. Incidentally, it may often be wiser not to dream of a complete elimination of the impulse toward aggression, but of its transformation or refinement. Gandhi felt that legitimate anger should be transmuted into constructive indignation.

Very often, it is not easy to perceive the sheer force of Love. During the early stages of his acquaintance with Gandhi's strategy of nonviolent resistance, Martin Luther King experienced "skepticism concerning the power of love." We should acknowledge that it is normal for any one of us to have such a reaction. King, however, overcame that skepticism, and came to see that the force of love and nonviolence amounts to a highly efficient and potent strategy.

Now, what we have to aim at doing is getting rid of systems based on violence. This can be achieved both on the international and the domestic planes. On the domestic plane, Martin Luther King saw that "the Christian doctrine of love, operating through the Gandhian method of nonviolence, is one of the most potent weapons available to oppressed people in their struggle for freedom."

On the international plane as well, nonviolence has its applications. In the early 1940s, at the height of World War II, a document was signed by two key leaders, insisting that, both from a moral viewpoint and from a pragmatic viewpoint, force should be abandoned as a way of solving differences between nations. Who were these two leaders? Idealists? They are not usually known as such. They were Franklin Roosevelt and Winston Churchill — who at Yalta in 1945 proved themselves to be fully realistic. However, at the time of writing the Atlantic Charter, they asserted in black and white their belief "that all of the nations of the world, for realistic as well as spiritual reasons, must come to the abandonment of the use of force."

Basically, how can we approach the everyday situations that we're faced with under conditions of conflict and violence? Let me suggest that there are five options:

1. To run away, which is cowardly. Incidentally, Gandhi had

the poorest opinion of cowardice in general, and even said that if there were only the choice of cowardice or fighting, he would be in favor of fighting. But he strongly questioned the fact that there is ever a choice between only these two.

2. To be neutral. How easy. How convenient and facile. But it is certainly not efficient from the Gandhian viewpoint, because it ignores both justice and injustice.

3. To capitulate, probably the worst option of the five.

4. To fight, of course, is another choice.

5. The last possibility, *which is for the brave*, is to respond nonviolently. And that involves inner courage. Toughness.

Now what does nonviolence mean? Nonviolence means not only resistance to violence in nonviolent ways, but a positive, constructive global strategy — what Gandhi referred to as his Constructive Program, encompassing a variety of sub-strategies. Gandhi has discussed nonviolence in a number of contexts, but perhaps most helpful is the formula he used to give when talking to rural audiences in India, where instead of more complex notions and concepts, he recommended five concerted endeavors. (For each of these points we have an analogous issue in our society today.)

First. Nonviolence, for Gandhi, meant working to do away with the injustices that existed for women in India. Western society wrestles with these problems in slightly different forms today. Our society is now dealing with the Equal Rights Amendment.

Second. Solve the injustices affecting the untouchables, or pariahs, or outcasts who were and are starkly present in

Indian society. But they are also present with us. There are the political refugees, the minorities, and others who are poor and homeless, in every major city. There are blacks living in ghettos while whites live in a different kind of ghetto in another part of town. By and large, Hispanics and other minorities do not intermingle with the mainstream of the population. There are other categories of vulnerable or 'marginal' humans whom many of us tend to overlook or reject: the terminally ill, the retarded, the advanced in age who are no longer integrated in the mainstream of society. Untouchables and outcasts are in every society.

Concerning the tendency of human nature to create outcasts, King had the following to say about the practice of racism:

> *"Racism is a philosophy based on a contempt for life. It is the arrogant assertion that one race is the center of value and object of devotion, before which other races must kneel in submission. It is the absurd dogma that one race is responsible for all the progress of history and along can assure the progress of the future. Racism is total estrangement. It separates not only bodies, but minds and spirits. Inevitably it descends to inflicting spiritual or physical homicide upon the out-group."*

Racism, or the proneness to create outcasts, is contrary to the ethic of love. Rejecting members of any human group is a form of violence. Love requires that we do not practice such rejection, but rather reach out to members of other cultural, social, and ethnic groups.

Third. Get involved in one particular and concrete economic activity that helps bring about greater sanity and fairness in the relationship between the poor and the rich.

As an example of such activity — for India Gandhi

advocated the use of the spinning wheel so that Indian peasants could generate some income, at a time when the majority of them were deprived of a means of earning a livelihood. In a similar vein, there are various policies we could pursue in the United States in keeping with the Gandhian inspiration: we can share our resources with the most impoverished people, by purchasing their products; or we could practice the strategies implemented by the Trusteeship Institute. (The Trusteeship Institute endeavors to bring about what it calls the *Third Way* — a new social order beyond capitalism and socialism. It does so by helping to spread the model of the Spanish-based Mondragon Cooperatives, by fostering socially responsible investments, and other forms of involvement. For more information, contact the Trusteeship Institute, Baker Road, Shutesbury, MA 01072.)

Fourth. Doing away with a serious problem that plagued Indian society then, addiction to drugs. In our culture, those who are active interpreting the Gandhi tradition view the media (i.e., television and the cinema) as a source of psychic numbing that is just as bad as addiction to other drugs. (In addition, through their unabashed portrayal or exaltation of violence, films like *Rambo* and many television programs very effectively foster violent behavior. The positive/creative solution of this issue is for us to learn to shake the psychic numbing that comes from an addiction to media, and learn to be more alert and alive through the practice of service, of right labor, of active nonviolence, and the other strategies presented in this little book.)

Fifth. Develop feelings of brotherhod toward members of other ethnic-cultural groups. In the case of India, it has meant brotherhood between Hindus, Muslims, and Sikhs.

In our land today it means cooperation and respect among ethnic and socio-economic groups, and doing away with the discrimination which oftentimes is practiced against Vietnamese refugees and others. In the Near East it means peace between Arabs and Jews.

Nonviolent resistance should appeal to love, to the law of love, to that spot inside each human being previously referred to. Where Tolstoy and Gandhi spoke of "the Law of Love," King talked in terms of a love ethic which should be at the center of one's life — the reality they all had in mind is the same. It follows from such a view that the nonviolent resister must avoid not only physical violence (e.g., shooting one's adversary) but also internal violence of the spirit (e.g., hating the adversary).

Because it is grounded in a love ethic, nonviolent resistance may not be, should not be, punitive. Gandhi stressed again and again that Indians should not try to punish the British for doing this and that. Following Gandhi, King stressed that the goal of nonviolent resistance is always redemption and reconciliation. It has been said of King (and could equally be said of his teacher Gandhi) that for him "The goal of nonviolence is not the humiliation or defeat of the opponent, but the winning of the enemy's friendship and understanding." Practicing nonviolence means trying to set things straight in a way that should be as patient, as educational, as composed, and as charitable as possible.

To be nonviolent does not mean merely not to fight. It means to muster considerable endurance and keep up the struggle: a persistent denunciation of injustice when there is injustice; a persistent disobedience to unjust laws. It means persistently, yet nonviolently and lovingly, pressuring an oppressor until the good in him or her recognizes our plight and responds to it. It also means, as Gandhi stressed, careful planning and clear strategy in order to provoke such a response. It means letting go as much as possible of our lust for control, power, and domination; it means our firm determination not to use others.

Closer to us in space and time than Gandhi, King vigorously reactivated and continued the practice of nonviolence. Some of the more striking aspects of King's views, as recently highlighted in an essay by William Watley, are the following: (1) For King, the conviction that the universe is on the side of justice "gives the nonviolent resister faith in the future and strength to accept suffering without retaliation." (2) The practice of nonviolence by Gandhi and King "assumes that there is social and economic power in non-cooperation and moral power in voluntary suffering for others." It has also been pointed out that King felt "the acceptance of suffering, rather than inflicting it on others, is itself a form a power, demoralizing to those who use violence without experiencing it in return and troublesome to the consciences of those who do not have an obvious vested interest in the maintenance of the system under attack" (John Swomley, Jr.).

Ultimately, the principle of nonviolence must be extended not only to human life but to the whole ecosphere — living and non-living things alike that all partake of the organic unity of our planet. The waste of resources, the pollution of air and water, the stripping of the land — all of these are also forms of lovelessness, disruption, and violence, and must be eliminated.

To practice nonviolence ("the weapon of the strong") requires considerable courage. At times, the conscience of the lucid and consistent nonviolent fighter leaves her or him no choice but to engage in civil disobedience actions, openly done with risk to the participant. Even such individual civil disobedience actions, however, are not adequate to the strategic needs of the extraordinary times through which our country is living. Beyond the fragmented efforts of individuals and specific groups, we are presently experiencing a crying need for a national nonviolent movement, with appropriately focused efforts.

A Note on Violence, War and Nonviolence

In the phenomenon known as war, nonviolence seems to be made impossible, and the nonviolent approach quixotic or irrelevant. In the Gandhian tradition there are four major explanations for war, four basic roots of war:

1. The first root is *greed* — for more possessions, or resources, or for new markets. This fact has both psychological and economic dimensions or implications. The industrial build-up for war has long been considered by many among the power elite and industrialists as a convenient solution to mass unemployment. (It certainly fulfilled that purpose in Nazi Germany in the 1930s.) Preparation for war and war itself syphon off the energies and attention of the most vigorous men in a nation, who would otherwise either be a burden to an economy that cannot absorb them, or be politically restless. With the hindsight that we should have today, condoning a war economy is a criminal course of action — it prepares for the unleashing of an untold amount of violence.

2. The second aspect of war is that, while military training does have some positive aspects from certain viewpoints, training for war and involvement in war strongly reinforce and develop a deep aggressive force that is present in all of us.

To be sure, there are diverse aspects to war and to the institution which keeps it going, the military. Alongside its main purpose (the conduct of offensive operations), there are other aspects to the military profession. Thus, soldiers in various countries have devoted certain amounts of time to activities directly fostering the welfare of citizens. An example is the work done in various countries by soldiers and officers belonging to a Corps of Engineers or similar army agencies, or by military personnel helping with the rescue of the population at times of disasters. (The latter function may be carried out by Air/Sea Rescue units, or in some countries by a National Guard.) Also, some aircraft of the U.S. Air Force, Marine, and Navy fly humanitarian flights (taking patients and accident victims to hospitals, conveying needed supplies of blood and organs), while the USAF is responsible for some aspects of the training of civilian pilots. Similarly, the Civil Air Patrol, an arm of the USAF, is used for search of aircraft that are overdue or missing.

Such examples of positive and timely involvement in operations ensuring the safety and welfare of citizens in need reveal how potentially useful the training provided by military-type discipline can be to help attain peaceful, constructive aims. In his book *The Power of Nonviolence*, Richard Gregg stressed the need for us to emulate the better, more positive aspects of military-type training and discipline and evolve an equivalent to them within the context of training in nonviolence. In the same way as we are confronted with the need for peace conversion economics, we need — within the framework of an integrated program for conversion to a nonviolent society — to consider gradual conversion of the purposes and energies behind traditional military training to constructive and peaceful purposes.

Along with that more positive aspect of military training, there is a more disturbing side to it. The basic purpose of the military is to prepare for and carry out war, and with that aim in mind it develops the brutish force that is sometimes active and sometimes dormant in us. It is this force which the military is immensely efficient at fostering, enhancing, and organizing. There is no denying that the military apparatus has achieved a considerable degree of sophistication at doing just that: transforming — as Tolstoy put it — men into not just animals, but into machines that will blindly obey orders and go out and kill. For some of us, to understand the Gandhian viewpoint on war, fighting, and the military may require a complete reorientation of our perspectives. It may not be easy to see that intervening militarily in a foreign country to meddle in its internal affairs is just another manifestation of brutish force; on a larger scale, this is just as bad as barging into my neighbor's backyard to tell him how to run his chicken-coop.

For many of us, it may be quite difficult to espouse the Tolstoyan-Gandhian perception which, quite simply put, is that a soldier is an extremely competent professional killer of other soldiers and civilians alike. If we look at the ratio of civilians killed in five successive wars — World War I, World War II, the Korean and Vietnam wars, the war in Central America — we see an escalating factor of civilian deaths.

In World War I there were 95 % military casualties and 5 % civilian casualties; in the Vietnam War, that proportion had reversed dramatically: there were 35 % civilian casualties and 65 % military casualties. Closer to home, some 100,000 Guatemalan civilians have been killed since 1954 within the framework of an "operation genocide" actively implemented by the military. These facts should make us completely rethink our notion of what war and the military are all about.

3. The third explanation of war is what we could call the cultural factor. There is a cultural deception. From childhood the notion has been instilled in us that patriotism is a good, necessary, and fine thing. Gandhi condemned exclusive or fanatic patriotism, and made it clear that he would only be a patriot if by being so he would not take away the slightest inch, one single iota, of the love and nurture that he owed to all other nations.

4. And finally, from the spiritual viewpoint, the stifling of the voice of conscience is the most disturbing occurrence in the military way of life as a result of war.

The question is sometimes asked: What would Gandhi have done in facing up to a Hitler? The answer is rather clear. If Gandhian principles had been employed and democracy had been fully implemented in Germany in the early 1930s, then Nazism would never have had the chance to emerge. Gandhi was far from being politically naive; he was a very astute politician, and he advocated participating very fully in the democratic process. Concerning the situation that developed in Germany after the Nazis had seized power, he wrote the Jewish philosopher Martin Buber to suggest specific strategies, based on his own somewhat inadequate (as he himself acknowledged) acquaintance with the German context.

The best time to stop wars is before they start. We hear threats of World War III. The time to avert such a disaster is now, by practicing love, not hate.

World Wars can grow out of regional wars. Regional wars can result from local injustices, lack of brotherhood, an insensitivity to our neighbors, from the ascendance of greed over love, from the bad habit of maintaining antagonisms against many persons and groups, from narrow-minded nationalism, from internecine religious fanaticism, from the ideological messianism of large and not-so-large countries.

The Beyond War movement deserves our gratitude for the clear and sharp logic it uses to analyze the reasons why *war is obsolete*, and to suggest that in consequence we should make the decision to reject war.

We will always be faced with the propensity in human nature to resort to warfare as a way of solving conflict. But there is a powerful alternate strategy advocated by Gandhi, which can be summed up as follows: Practice the Law of Love; insist that the institutions around which our life is organized apply nonviolence; and re-train ourselves to become nonviolent — that is, to learn to solve conflict without resorting to violence. (For concrete applications, consult Marshall B. Rosenberg's *A Model for Nonviolent Communication,* and Mark Juergensmeyer's *Fighting with Gandhi* — see "Suggested Readings".)

> *Refrain from the violence of fist, tongue, or heart.*
> — *Volunteer Commitment Card, Alabama Christian Movement for Human Rights, 1960*

Solution:

Practice the Law of Love. Love means thoughtful attentiveness; therefore, practice creative listening to the other's side. In dealing with an opponent, search actively for areas of mutual interests; on the basis of these interests, build projects to encourage the development of increasing mutual trust. Use **negotiation, arbitration**, and other **conflict-solving methods**, at local, national, international levels. Fully utilize and improve existing dispute resolution systems between nations so that war is not the only option. Freeze and reverse the arms race. Cut the military budget. Practice nonviolence as an active struggle. Actively pursue alternatives to military intervention. Support human freedom and dignity by ending foreign military intervention (interfering in another country's internal affairs is a form of violence). Support human freedom and dignity at home by endorsing civil liberties (not granting such liberties is also a form of violence). Persistently denounce and oppose injustice.

4
CONCILIATION / RECONCILIATION, NEGOTIATION, MEDIATION

"The Law is not Higher than the Law of Love"

> *Problem:*
>
> Alienation in relation to people, society. Alienation from basic, warm, interpersonal relating to people. Exclusive **reliance on intermediaries** (police, judiciary) to avoid dealing directly with people, with potential conflicts. Systematic **legalistic approach**.

"The purpose of the law is to defend the weak from the strong." This perception of the British philosopher John Stuart Mill was shared by Gandhi when, after graduating from the bar in England, he practiced law for twenty years, mostly in South Africa. Gandhi felt that the lawyer's true function was to unite parties that have become estranged. He toiled unceasingly as an attorney who came to the rescue of the poor and defenseless (especially indentured Indian laborers). Gandhi made maximum use of the possibilities afforded by the law and judiciary apparatus to bring about greater justice in South Africa.

However, he made scathing statements about the fiendishness and brutishness of the mentality which uses the judiciary to practice aggression rather than love. He felt that for two disagreeing parties to go to law could often be "another form of the exhibition of brute force." Gandhi's thoughts on this subject are a variation on the injunction found in the Sermon on the Mount. Do not take your brother to law, but rather make things up with him prior to — and rather than — appearing before a judge. We have become blind to the extent that going to court for handling human situations pervades our way of life.

The reason for Gandhi's — and Jesus' — misgivings about the systematic or reflex-like recourse to the judiciary is that fear, constraint, and force will never achieve justice. Having recourse to the judiciary as a form of the Law of Aggression rules out the chance for one to practice the Law of Love.

A very fundamental alternate to automatic or systematic recourse to the judiciary is the practice of conciliation. One of the principles underlying Gandhi's strong commitment to achieving conciliation was later taken up by Ted Crawford in his method for "Sharing and Exploring of Differences" as a path to peace: "While sharing differences, have enough flexibility to consider (from the outset) moving toward a third position."

Pioneering work on the value of negotiation and putting oneself in the right frame of mind for the achieving of conciliation has been conducted by the Harvard Negotiation Project and reported on by Roger Fisher and William Ury in *Getting to Yes: Negotiating Agreement Without Giving In.* The Harvard Negotiation Project generated such activities as the Negotiation Seminar and the Conflict Clinic. The Project teaches such techniques, skills, and devices as: "principled negotiation" (as opposed to both "hard negotiation" and "soft negotiation"); better communication; using "negotiation jujitsu;" and "taming the hard bargainer." Fisher and Ury show their readers how to move away from the all-too-frequent notion of individualistic winning at all costs — while learning to win such prized rewards as a better and more efficient way to negotiate, and the satisfaction of working out a solution to a shared problem. From a Gandhian viewpoint, all such efforts are "skillful means" or devices used to implement the Law of Love.

As Tolstoy put it, "There can't be any sanctity and law higher than the sanctity of the Law of Love to one's neighbor." In clear cases when the letter of any human law or the way it is being enforced flagrantly violates a higher value — the practice of Love, then we are in duty bound to consider seriously which our conscience would have us obey — the questionable letter of a written code of law, or the Law of Love.

Instead of the formal/legalistic approach to human beings which has tended to prevail in much of our way of life in the West, and in other parts of the world, we should practice as much direct dialogue as possible with the "opponent." Echoing these Gandhian concerns, United States Chief Justice Warren E. Burger recently called the American legal system "too costly, too painful, too destructive, and too inefficient for a truly civilized people." We should use a variety of possible approaches dictated to us by our hearts and minds, including negotiation, conciliation, mediation, sharing of differences, co-responsibility, and the co-creation of a valid and creative compromise which is a recognition of the element of truth within "the other" out there.

In Chief Justice Burger's words, "Trials by the adversarial contest must in time go the way of the ancient trial by battle and blood."

> *Readiness to understand and appreciate the other person's point of view is the very essence of the search for Truth.*
>
> — *An Indian disciple of Gandhi*

Solution:

De-institutionalize what should be direct interpersonal contact. Abandon formal/legalistic approach to divergences and conflicts with fellow humans. Practice as much **direct dialogue** as possible with our "opponent." Use negotiation, **conciliation, mediation**, arbitration, sharing of differences, co-creating, co-responsibility.

5
PARTICIPATION IN GOVERNMENT

Problem:

Alienation in relation to our government. And thinking, "It's the government's job to do the job, to decide for us."

Big government is alienating, depersonalizing.

We must train ourselves to examine the institutions we have created. If a governing body, a militia, a road or highway repair service, does not achieve what our best judgment, our consciences, our moral selves, want it to achieve, we must re-evaluate why we as citizens made it possible for such a service to come into being. It is wrong to assume the judiciary or the military or government as a whole, stands for justice or peace.

All too often, government has become a convenient device for the delegation of our responsibilities, and just a convenient abstraction — insofar as it takes away from individuals certain responsibilities, privileges, and functions, claiming that it will take them over, thereby exonerating us from any need to feel concern about such responsibilities.

One important concern we should have in the area of government is to reverse the trend toward excessive centralization, to make sure that individual economic/administrative/political units or entities are manageable in size. Kirkpatrick Sale's *Dwellers in the Land: The Bioregional Vision*, which has already been mentioned, contains important insights on this score. An especially valuable compact statement of the Gandhian strategy of judicious regionalism is the booklet by Gora (G. Ramachandra Rao) entitled *Why Gram-Raj* (a title which may be interpreted as, "Regional Autonomy, Gandhian Style: A Program for Socio-Economic-Administrative Conversion"); its application of the Gandhian insights into the situation in India would need to be translated into terms applicable to the Western context.

Effectively conveying our wishes and values to our representatives and elected leaders is a complex task, considering the discrepancy between the best values we believe in and the notions or principles by which these representatives are guided (and this is true of most Western, Communist bloc, and Third World countries). Representatives and leaders, for the most part, are drawn from the ranks of the highly privileged and/or meritocracy, and are motivated by a dysfunctional philosophy of life, which operates on achievement and reward principles. Unless and until we insist that our leaders adhere to more enlightened values, we are always voting for men who are the products of a general social dysfunction. Elected representatives or leaders who are "successful" under the present system would have a difficult time accepting the need for far-reaching changes in the direction of the saner values advocated by Gandhi and a few others.

We must make sure that through representation of our opinions, through our votes and actions, government agencies achieve their original purpose — the administration of a required service in accordance with our aims and values. If they no longer do so they no longer deserve our support. The time may have come to think of another approach. The Gandhian approach.

With considerable lucidity, Gandhi cautioned us, stating, "The State represents violence in a concentrated and organized form. . . . as the State is a soulless machine, it can never be weaned from violence to which it owes its very existence." Unless we constantly make an effort to convey to our government the best and loftiest notions instilled in us by our conscience, the soulless violence within the machine will prevail. At the same time as he denounced the violence within the machine of the State, Gandhi firmly believed in the need for us to work for the moral and political well-being of the nation of which we are a part. (In fact, that belief was so definite in him that it led to — largely ill-conceived — reproaches on the part of both Tolstoy and Erik Erikson that Gandhi pandered unduly to the cause of Hindu patriotism.)

Gandhi invited us to develop enough boldness to speak up to our government and its leaders when necessary. This can be done through letters and calls to our legislators, through tax resistance, or in other ways that forcefully convey our concerns. In the contemporary context for us, the words we should boldly speak to our government on the basis of inspiration from Gandhi might be as follows:

"Please do not draft anyone into the military or maintain a standing army in my name. The sole purpose of a military establishment is to prepare and execute killing — this it achieves by systematically breaking and humiliating army recruits, so they will kill ruthlessly; and I want no part of such an operation. There are far better things that trained, skilled and organized people can do with their lives. Kindly refrain from threatening or bullying any other nations or peoples in my name; there is plenty of fear and pain in the world already, and I see no reason to add to it. Do not maintain any more dictatorships in my name. Please do not build or stockpile a ridiculously exaggerated quantity of weapons in my name; I do not want such 'protection.' Even if some feel that the violent repression of foreigners (e.g., Nicaraguan civilians) is somehow essential to the 'security' of my country, I demand that it cease; I do not wish to benefit from such horror, and I do formally repudiate and reject any and all 'protection' such repression may afford." (Based on a statement by Greg Johnson.)

In essence, we should take our share of responsibility in the running of our own country. Focused political effort sustained by nonviolent values can dissolve layers of apathy, and overcome the current political crisis in our country. As the need occurs, we should have the courage to work in the halls of government and courts of law to exercise our duties as participating citizens. As need be, we should also have the courage to undertake protests, boycotts, and other acts of civil disobedience such as were practiced to bring about the independence of the American colonies. As Gandhi's foremost Indian disciple Vinoba Bhave (1895-1982) insisted, the power of the people has to be awakened, so that the people can rule more effectively (rather than entrusting this task entirely to an often alienating entity, the state). And after all, Vinoba was echoing Thomas Jefferson's statement, "I know of no safe repository of the ultimate power of society but the people."

The citizen is the sovereign, who appoints the government.
— An Indian disciple of Gandhi

Solution:

Participate in the democratic process. Take responsibility for our government. Think: "The state is our state; we must participate in running it." Support the government only if it allows *fair representation*. De-bureaucratize life. Practice **decentralization**. **Small is beautiful**, small preserves a human scale, a human spirit. Support communication between government and citizens, based on sharing (as opposed to adversarial approaches).

6
EDUCATION / RE-EDUCATION / RE-EVALUATION OF VALUES

Problem:

Alienation from others caused by the educational process. Education which merely fosters maximum gathering of information and competence. Education which is based on an antagonistic spirit of **competition**. Education which fosters a random, casual, egotistic, happy-go-lucky approach to civic realities and responsibilities.

Nonviolence is something which has to be instilled in us by careful and thoughtful education. Gandhian education — as practiced in the various schools and colleges founded by Mahatma Gandhi since the 1920s — develops three aspects of the individual: the mind, the heart, and the skill to use one's hands. The child knows with his mind, loves with his heart, and creates with his hands. Unless we provide outlets for all three and training in all three areas, the child has a lopsided education.

The competitiveness which pervades most Western and Asian schools is excessive. Reacting against this, Gandhi said that unless and until we learn to get away from that spirit of competition and create a dynamic and cooperative spirit, we are not educating others or ourselves in the best sense of the term. If anything, contemporary American education is even more narrowly professional and specialization-oriented than British and Indian schools in Gandhi's time, and it is clear that Gandhi did not approve of such an approach.

Children in Gandhian schools don't accumulate learning as many people accumulate assets or riches — they don't learn for the purpose of being first or winning a competition, at the expense of others. Rather than being acquisitive/competitive, Gandhian education is cooperative. It prepares the individual to fit into a non-exploitative social structure. While it endorses the development of intellectual abilities, Gandhian education agrees with Albert Schweitzer that love is the supreme knowledge, and views as the highest value the creation of a non-exploitive and loving framework of relationships with others.

Also, whereas the mainstream culture is markedly argument-oriented in its teaching and fostering of opinionated debate and polemics, the Gandhian strategy requires that we do not espouse such an adversarial practice, but rather foster agreement-oriented dialogue, conducive to the establishment of harmony. Beyond a clear and frank initial statement or acknowledgement of differences, all the energies of those engaged in dialogue should go toward solving or overcoming these differences, rather than harping exclusively on the originally perceived divergence.

Gandhian "Basic Education" (or "New Education" — *Nai talim*) fosters self-sufficiency. With that aim in mind, students do their own laundry, work in the kitchen, sweep and scrub, practice gardening, weaving, pottery, carpentry — as well as learn the three R's and acquire knowledge of essential academic subjects. In summation, "Basic Education" is: 1) child-centered or learner-centered; 2) dynamic; 3) cooperative; 4) nonviolent; 5) geared toward the acquisition of self-sufficiency.

Education is given to children for definite and specific purposes, but as adults we have to continue training and educating ourselves. Part of that training could be the fostering of the specific disciplines which Richard Gregg advocates in *The Power of Nonviolence* — the practice of reading and discussion; silent meditation; manual work (aimed at developing Gandhian self-reliance); music and group singing (a category under which we could foster the "freedom songs" of current times); the systematic practice of nonviolence in small, everyday matters; the cultivation of sentiments which lead to nonviolence (tolerance, patience, humility, love of truth, love of people, faith in the ultimate possibilities of human nature). Martin Luther King also felt strongly about the need for us to undertake a revaluation of values or a reconditioning of our minds and hearts in the light of a commitment to love and nonviolence.

From a Gandhian viewpoint, education is a benefit to which all should have access — and in this realm as well, sharing with the destitute (that cardinal precept of Gandhian ethics) applies. Those who are "destitute" (Gandhi's term) or "disadvantaged" (King's term) are referred to as "the oppressed" by the contemporary theoretician of education Paulo Freire. For Freire, "the oppressed" are those who are subjected to repressive or violent treatment — including repressive or non-liberating pedagogical approaches. What Freire refers to as an authentic or liberating type of education is in effect what Gandhi advocated — nonviolent education. For Freire non-repressive or liberating education is dialogue oriented, is education as the practice of freedom — as opposed to education as the practice of domination or violence.

The comradeship or communion with the oppressed which Freire advocates in his book *Pedagogy of the Oppressed* is akin to Gandhian identification with the destitute. When Freire says that true solidarity with the oppressed — or "conversion to the people" or "committing oneself to the people" — is achieved only in an act of love toward them, he is expressing a feeling that is central to Gandhi's approach. According to Gandhi, such solidarity with the oppressed and destitute needs to be practiced in every sphere of action, including education.

All of these endeavors should be viewed as necessary components of an integrated and efficient training in nonviolence — of a training in the Law of Love. A fair measure of training along these lines is essential if we want to achieve the extent of personal and societal transformation required of us today for our world to achieve greater sanity, and to ensure our survival.

In the mainstream of day-to-day living within just about any context or country, there has been and is an overwhelming tendency for individuals and groups not to see their own faults and to blame others. Training in nonviolence means training in countering this tendency, training in achieving understanding of mutual diverse positions, and training in solving conflict. As has been pointed out in a contemporary formulation of the nonviolent approach such as the message of the Beyond War movement, if we are to survive, then a complete reorientation of our psychic energies is necessary to enable a continuing, global process of education and re-education. This would be the most monumental educational endeavor ever undertaken by the human species.

Solution:

Foster humane and balanced teaching. Develop **mind** and **heart** and **skill** in using our hands. Teach youngsters and other learners to think logically, ask questions, criticize, and recognize untruth. Re-educate and retrain ourselves. Develop intentional, systematic **training in nonviolence**, based on Gandhian practices. Practice shared responsibility training.

I would develop in the child his hands, his brain, and his soul. The hands have almost atrophied. The soul has been altogether ignored.

— *Gandhi*

7
SHARING OF RESOURCES
Dealing with Poverty and Wealth

Problem:

Gross inequality exists in distribution of resources. There are severe **extremes of poverty and wealth.**

Proper handling of the distribution of resources between rich and poor is a fundamental part of Gandhi's strategy for peace and justice. Time and again, Gandhi stressed the link between the issue of poverty, wealth, and resource management, on the one hand, and a peace based on nonviolence, on the other. For example, he pointed out that, "A nonviolent system of government is clearly an impossibility so long as the wide gulf between the rich and hungry millions persists."

In formulations which are only slightly different from that stark Gandhian statement, an essentially similar point has been made by various contemporaries — e.g., by Pope Paul VI when he stated, "If you want peace, work for justice," and by the American Catholic bishops in a recent pastoral letter in which they pointed out that fair and just policies to ensure the economic welfare of all, especially the underprivileged, are crucial to the establishment of peace in the world. Also, there is King's expression in 1963 of the hopes of America: "I have a dream that one day this nation will rise up and live out the true meaning of its creed, 'We hold these truths to be self-evident — that all men are created equal.'" All of this is echoed in a recent statement

---

by the Tanzanian leader Julius Nyerere, "Peace is a product of justice. There is no peace in the world without an effort to deal with poverty and injustice."

The statements by Gandhi and these recent variations convey a clear message: If injustice prevails, then discontent or hostility ensues, and in discontent and hostility are the seeds of social and political unrest or upheaval — and peace cannot prevail.

We have to make a considerable effort in order to perceive clearly the relationship between peace and social justice. In various contexts, that relationship is not always visible to the naked eye. Yet, there is much that lucid scrutiny reveals: All around us, situations exist whereby excessive poverty in the lives of some is triggered and caused by a mathematically proportionate amount of excessive wealth in the hands of others. The superfluous wealth of some is the most important cause of the dire poverty of others. In some contexts, such disparity arises as a result of political systems which allow dominating hereditary concentrations of power, or concentrations due to violence; most universally, it arises because of the greed and lust for economic domination which so often prevails in human nature. (Economically speaking, there is no reason for us to conclude that greed is a necessary part of human nature; it is a worthwhile assumption that greed is in part the result of centuries of scarcity — but now, for the first time, technology can produce enough for all, and we should expect that greed can abate. Psychologically speaking, within the Buddhist world view greed is one of the three raging fires which consume humans; it needs to be put out for us to attain balance, harmony and true fulfillment.)

Gandhi felt strongly that, mathematically speaking, there

is a direct relationship between extremes of poverty on the one hand, and extremes of wealth on the other. (As another twentieth-century thinker put it, "The substance of the rich man's joy is the poor man's suffering.") A direct relationship between extremes of economic oppression and excessive crushing toil on the one hand, and on the other, excessive luxury, superfluity, and idle wastefulness. Between excessive want and excessive surfeit. Similarly, there is a direct relationship between extremes of submission on the one hand, and on the other, extremes of domination. Gandhi felt strongly about this mutual causality and the resulting unfair distribution; he recognized the part that violence plays in it, even the concealed violence of unjust laws.

This is not a viewpoint that is peculiar to Gandhi. Jesus made it plain that having many possessions is a hindrance to spiritual growth, and drastic cutting down is required for any significant advancement or progress to occur. He too was concerned with the contrast between the rich and poor, with the relationship between extremes of wealth and poverty, and the underlying mutual causality. This is driven home by the stark paradox, in the Gospel of Luke, of the logically interrelated outcries, "Blessed are you the poor . . ." and "Woe to you the rich, for you have received your consolation." And these statements have deep resonance within the Judaism of the Prophets. The fact that the mainstream Christian tradition has been uncomfortable with that dimension of the Sermon on the Mount, and has tended to gloss over it, accounts for the lack of responsiveness to it of many Christians today. But numerous Christian thinkers over the centuries, such as Fathers of the Christian Church Saint Jerome and Saint John Chrysostom, reverberated such statements from the Gospels.

Thus, Jerome, four centuries after Christ, came up with a quite disturbing rephrasing of the point made by Jesus when he said that no man can be wealthy unless this wealth has come to him either from injustice or from being an heir to injustice. This statement may sound extreme at first, making it terribly uncomfortable for those of us who have been born and raised in the lap of luxury or who have acquired more wealth than we need. At the same time, some feel that the wealth they have accumulated is the legitimate reward for their labor. As a matter of fact, it seems to be the case that certain individuals have gained great wealth who provided needed products or services, while charging non-exploitative rates for these.

In any case, both Gandhi and Jesus conveyed to the well-to-do that enjoyment of the fruits of our labor is legitimate *as long as we practice an attitude of stewardship and trusteeship,* and acknowledge the responsibility which the possession of these resources places upon us. At the same time, Gandhi (again echoing Jesus) warned that the possession of riches was a potential "hindrance to real growth."

Gandhi time and again talked about the "wide gulf" separating the very rich from the hungry millions. He felt that such a situation contained the germs of a revolutionary scenario. A blueprint for revolution. Feeling that much violence is constantly being perpetrated towards the poor, Gandhi actually described poverty as a state of violence that we have allowed to come into being. In practice, public opinion focuses so much on specific *acts* of violence, such as acts of terrorism, that we overlook the existence of persistent, institutionalized *states* of violence — another significant manifestation of violence in everyday life.

Gandhi's perception of the workings of that

poverty/wealth interconnectedness has been corroborated by the feelings of a number of enlightened minds in the West. Thus, one of the greatest American Christian activists, Dorothy Day, talked about the cold war being waged between the rich and the poor; and King was very vocal in denouncing that war, and highlighting "the tenacious poverty which so paradoxically exists in the midst of plenty."

In this day and age when statistics are readily available, we have a general idea of the figures and proportions underlying that tension or "war" between poverty and plenty. We know that about one-quarter of humankind functions in a self-accelerating cycle of affluence, while the remaining three-quarters are plunged in a quagmire of poverty, of misery, from which they cannot extricate themselves. We know that about 20% of the world's population, in the wealthiest countries, use about 80% of the resources. We know that, as Pope John Paul II recently recalled, the gap between the "rich north" (the Northern Hemisphere) and the "poor south" (the Southern Hemisphere) is constantly growing. Gandhi holds before us the direct, necessary causal relationship between the extremes. (The fact that the gap between rich and poor is constantly widening — as is well documented by economists, and was mentioned by the Pope in the same statement — should not surprise us, if we consider that the violence of the system is a self-accelerating mechanism.)

What do we do when faced with such a situation? Gandhi suggested four solutions, four lines of endeavor:

1. *Simplify our lifestyle and practice intentional frugality.* Basically, what Gandhi calls upon us to do is to simplify for both economic and moral reasons. To change our lifestyle in the direction of frugality (which is akin to the "poverty"

mentioned in the Sermon on the Mount) and intentional simplification in terms of energy and resource usage, the "natural way" of doing things, and more contact with the people around us. In the past fifteen or twenty years a number of authors have stressed the intentional practice of frugality, as both the morally and economically appropriate course of action. Among the most significant of these advocates of frugality are Duane Elgin, the author of *Voluntary Simplicity*, and David E. Shi, who recently published the book, *The Simple Life: Plain Living and High Thinking in American Culture.*

Gandhi stated: ". . . some people accumulate wealth, regarding their greed as their religion. . . . In proportion as we make our outer life more and more elaborate, we harm our moral progress, and we injure true religion." (According to Gandhi, true religion consists in direct "service of the helpless" and in whatever fosters that aim.) He felt that in proportion as we make our external life more elaborate, more consumption-oriented, we alter for the worse the distribution of resources in the world, and cut ourselves off from our brothers and sisters who have to get by with the minimum.

2. *Practice Trusteeship/Stewardship.* Gandhi said we should consider ourselves as trustees. That is, we should consider ourselves responsible as trustees for all the goods and the riches, the facilities and the good things that have been given or *entrusted* to us by a greater Cosmic Will or Providence. These resources are not really ours but everyone's. They are gifts that we have been entrusted with to share with others in need. Gandhi's notion of trusteeship is grounded in law, from his training as a lawyer in London and his subsequent legal practice for decades. His conception of trusteeship is also closely related to the "stewardship" of the Gospels (a

text which influenced him directly); there, in numerous parables, Jesus called on his listeners to be good stewards.

Gandhian-style trusteeship means practicing a community approach to property and a joint ownership of resources. (It might be mentioned that Gandhi himself, from middle life on, was no longer content with the mere practice of trusteeship, but went beyond, to the practice of dispossession and renunciation of most of his earthly belongings, and experienced considerable joy and liberation in so doing. His essential motivation in taking this step was the desire to achieve fuller *identification* with the destitute, and to experience a bond of authentic brotherhood with them; such a motivation had been that of St. Francis of Assisi before him.)

3. *Give the underprivileged the right to work* — and to a kind of work which allows for reasonable fulfillment. As opposed to practicing philanthropy, as opposed to giving out alms and nurturing the illusion that we are practicing generosity, Gandhi advocated the practice of basic justice — that is, the extent of justice we, the overprivileged, need to practice before we can think of going one step further to generosity. Although he acknowledged there was an urgent need to help the destitute, he believed that in due time philanthropy should disappear. Basic justice demands that we, the overprivileged, provide the poor and helpless with better job training and/or better work opportunities — such is the Gandhian conception of fostering self-sufficiency or self-help (*swadeshi*). In other words, helping the underprivileged to help themselves is the greatest gift we can give them.

4. *Generally, learn to share and give.* Practice sharing and giving as a form of selfless service. (For more specific suggestions, see "What Can I Do?", numbers 37-40.)

A Note on Violence, Poverty and Wealth

As pointed out by Adam Curle, an insightful British Quaker, the violence of the system in our western society deprives those at the lower end of the socio-economic scale of what is necessary to fulfillment, both materially and — since they are made to feel inferior and insecure — psychologically.

Curle brings up some basic facts. Being deprived of a certain range of medical services, the poor have a lower life expectancy. They have an infant mortality rate four times that of the rich. Those born into the upper echelon of the socio-economic scale are seven times less likely than the poor to leave school early. Subsequently, they are much more likely to go on to college and get a degree which will make them *twenty times* more likely than someone with a high school diploma or similar qualifications to earn top salaries which will place them among the ten percent of the population who possess about ninety percent of the wealth. Curle's facts concern Great Britain, while we know in substance they are true of other Western countries. (See Adam Curle, *True Justice: Quaker Peace Makers and Peace Making*, London, 1981.)

> *I am proposing . . . that . . . America launch a broad-based and gigantic Bill of Rights for the Disadvantaged . . .*
>
> — *Martin Luther King, Jr.*

Solution:

Practice love grounded in **economic justice**. Establish a fairer and saner **balance of resources** in the world. Change systems of production and distribution. Co-create "new" solutions so that mutual benefits result. Build a society that provides for basic human needs such as adequate housing, health, education, jobs in humane working conditions, and a safe environment. A society that provides equal opportunities to develop the fullest potential of each individual. Simplify our own lifestyle; practice frugality. Regard possessions in the light of trusteeship. Be fair in allowing the underprivileged the right to work. Learn to **share** — to **give** — to practice **generosity** on a daily basis; make these activities part of our lifestyle.

SUMMARY

Gandhi had his own vision of the future of India . . . That vision was of a new social order — different from the capitalist, socialist, communist orders of society. A nonviolent society, a society based on love and human values, a decentralized, self-governing, non-exploitative, cooperative society. Gandhi gave that society the name of Sarvodaya — i.e., a society in which the good of all is achieved. . . . A total [Gandhian] revolution will bring about fundamental changes in the social, economic, political, cultural, educational, and moral spheres.

— Jayaprakash Narayan,
Indian politician, leading disciple of Gandhi

All people are members of the same family, endowed with a moral conscience. We, as members of this family, must work to bring about equality where there is inequality, justice when there is injustice, and peace when there is threat of war, by living the Law of Love.

Concrete steps can be taken daily to create more peace around us. If we are willing to give up holding antagonisms toward persons or groups, we can de-fuse aggression at every opportunity and approach closer understanding with our family, neighbors, and friends, and thus create an atmosphere of love.

We can donate our time in the form of selfless service in community work, action groups, and social work.

We must move in the direction of voluntary simplicity to put an end to the great division between the rich and poor.

An evaluation of the institutions controlling our lives must be made to ensure they represent what the best in us wants them to achieve.

Our schools must provide the education for our children

to know, to create, and to love — and that aim of education must be continued in the life of adults. At the same time as we un-learn competitive and aggressive ways, we must continue educating and training ourselves and each other to practice attitudes and actions which generate peace within us and around us.

These different aspects of the overall Gandhian strategy for peace and justice are closely interrelated. Non-achievement of any one aspect is a potential hindrance to the achievement of the other aspects. Achieving one aspect or goal fosters the achievement of the other goals in Gandhi's overall, integrated program. Achieving decentralization, restructuring society along non-exploitative and cooperative lines, practicing frugality, sharing resources, having recourse to negotiation and conciliation — all these activities and practices are an integral part of his overall, global vision of a social order based on love and nonviolence.

And these endeavors consist of intensely concrete and practical steps, which each one of us can undertake. Today.

WHAT ABOUT GETTING STARTED TODAY? Specific suggestions are provided in "What Can I Do?" beginning on the next page.

WHAT CAN I DO?
A Guide for Action — Practical Steps

"Almost anything you do will seem insignificant, but it is very important that you do it."

— Mahatma Gandhi

These suggestions are divided into seven categories, corresponding to the seven areas of the Gandhian program. Review carefully as many as possible of these suggestions, and decide for yourself which ones you personally find feasible and reasonable to practice, on a daily, weekly, or monthly basis (making your choice in the light of your circumstances). Once your choice is made, try to make a firm commitment for a period of, say, two months. Declare your commitment to the other service-oriented individuals with whom you meet (if you decide following suggestion No. 34 below). Every two months, review your progress, and confirm or revise your commitment.

1: SELFLESS SERVICE

1. "Seek to perform regular service for others and for the world" (Volunteer Commitment Card, Alabama Christian Movement for Human Rights, 1960). Actively search for action groups and institutions in your area which are involved in some form of selfless service (i.e., unpaid, non-self-seeking service), community work, or social work (providing shelter for the homeless, job training, providing emergency meals, etc.). These groups may be secular or church related. The American Friends Service Committee branches and Catholic Worker Houses are examples.

Write NTL Institute, P.O. Box 9155, Rosslyn Station, Arlington, VA 22209, for a listing of volunteer service agencies.

2. Contact at least one or two local branches of such

organizations, when possible, and find out more about their programs. Then get involved in your preferred choice, giving half a day or an evening of your week to some form of selfless service, either through an organization, or directly to a needy party.

3. Give two, three, four or more weeks of your time every year to selfless service in the form of a special project such as American Friends Service Committee work in Mexico, a Habitat for Humanity project in Appalachia or Guatemala, a community development project in Costa Rica, a rural development project in India, or work with the Christian Service Corps, headquartered in Washington, D.C.

4. If you have appropriate skills (educational, technical, agricultural, medical, etc.), consider volunteering with the Peace Corps, 806 Connecticut Avenue, Washington, D.C. 20526. For more information on various other forms of volunteer service, consult Marjorie Cohen's *The Comprehensive Guide to Voluntary Service in the U.S. and Abroad* (Intercultural Press, P.O. Box 768, Yarmouth, ME 04096) or Eva Schindler-Rainman's *The Volunteer Community: Creative Use of Human Resources.* Another important resource is the book, *How Can I Help?*, by Ram Dass and P. Gorman (New York: Knopf, 1985).

5. See other nationals, and "aliens" generally, as our brothers and sisters. Participate in the work of an organization promoting the idea of the interdependence of all peoples, such as Planetary Citizens, 1150 Chestnut St., Menlo Park, CA 94025.

2: RIGHT AND FAIR LABOR

6. If you are a white-collar worker, or live a life of relative leisure with little or no involvement in physical activity, get involved in some form of manual work, even if only in a small way. View that work as a chance to be closer to the plight of the many millions who have no choice but to practice often unpalatable or oppressive forms of physical labor.

7. In the light of Gandhian principles, review your current bread-winning occupation. Maybe you'll wish to consider some other form of activity, perhaps changing to a means of livelihood which serves a more useful purpose in society, or doing something else on an occasional or seasonal basis, such as summer work.

8. If at all possible, grow a vegetable garden, even if it is in a small backyard, or on a balcony. (Write this organic gardening publisher: Rodale Press, 33 E. Minor St., Emmaus, PA 18049.) Plant one tree a year, for the next five years. Consider getting in touch with the Tree People, 12601 Mulholland Dr., Beverly Hills, CA 90210.

9. Get involved in fostering some aspect of what E.F. Schumacher has termed "appropriate" or "intermediate" technology. (Contact: Intermediate Technology, 556 Santa Cruz Avenue, Menlo Park, CA 92045; Appropriate Technology Development Association, P.O. Box 311, Gandhi Bhawan, Lucknow — 226001, Uttar Pradesh, India.) Consider boycotting inappropriate technology. Achieve greater harmony with the environment by not exploiting it; by recycling paper, compost, etc.

10. Consider supporting the Jobs with Peace Campaign, which brings together people in local communities and

national organizations across the country who are working for more money in their communities and less for the military. (People in 71 cities have voted in favor of initiatives making this demand.) Write: Jobs with Peace, 2822 S. Western Ave., Los Angeles, CA 90018.

11. Investigate possibilities for economic conversion planning. Write the Center for Economic Conversion (formerly Mid-Peninsula Conversion Project), 222C View St., Mountain View, CA 94041. You may wish to take some of the following concrete steps toward Peace Conversion planning: work for local peace conversion initiatives, such as the "Jobs with Peace" resolution in Los Angeles; contact local chairs of the boards of industries engaged in defense work and urge peace conversion conferences and workshops with management, labor, and community represented; push for the development of a peace conversion plan in every defense plant; interview local military representatives and ask them what they are going to do when the arms race ends.

12. Support the efforts of Cesar Chavez and his co-workers on behalf of fair working and living conditions for migrant farm workers in this country. In this connection, you might consider supporting the current grape boycott. Write: Cesar Chavez, United Farm Workers/AFL-CIO, La Paz, Keene, CA 93531.

3: NONVIOLENCE

13. Every day, make a concrete gesture, or take a concrete step which will help enhance peace around you. At every opportunity defuse aggression and antagonisms within and around you and strive for mutual understanding and

harmony. Practice the "magic formula for resolving conflicts" proposed by Peace Pilgrim (190?-1981): *"Have as your objective the resolving of the conflict, not the gaining of advantage."* And her magic formula for *avoiding* conflicts: *"Be concerned that you do not offend, not that you are not offended."* Spread the message of Peace Pilgrim by contacting: Friends of Peace Pilgrim, 43480 Cedar Ave., Hemet, CA 92344.

14. Make some commitment of your time and energies to work for a group which is pursuing peace. Some suggestions: Beyond War, 222 High St., Palo Alto, CA 94301; The Peace Project, 511 Cayuga St., Santa Cruz, CA 95062; The Great Peace March for Global Nuclear Disarmament, Inc., 1431 Ocean Ave., Suite B, Santa Monica, CA 90401; American Peace Test, P.O. Box 26725, Las Vegas, NV 89126.

Other such groups are: American Friends Service Committee, Catholic Worker Houses, Christophers, Clergy and Laity Concerned, Coalition for a New Foreign and Military Policy, Council for a Livable World, Fellowship of Reconciliation, Jobs with Peace, Mobilization for Survival, Movement for a New Society, New Jewish Agenda, Nuclear Weapons Freeze Campaign, Pax Christi USA, Physicians for Social Responsibility (and other similar groups such as Educators for Social Responsibility, etc.), SANE, Sojourners Peace Ministry, Southern Christian Leadership Conference, Union of Concerned Scientists, Unitarian Universalist Association, United Church of Christ Peace Advocacy Project, War Resisters League, Women's Action for Nuclear Disarmament, Women's International League for Peace and Freedom, A.J. Muste Memorial Institute. (For addresses, and a full listing of peace groups, write the publishers of *American Peace Directory*, Institute for Defense and Disarmament

Studies, 2001 Beacon St., Brookline, MA 02146; or write the United Peace Network, P.O. Box 1314, Santa Ana, CA 92702.)

15. Help foster awareness of the escalation of nuclear buildup and what can be done about it by disseminating copies of such convenient manuals as: *The Hundredth Monkey* by Ken Keyes, Jr. (contact: Vision Books, 790 Commercial Ave., Coos Bay, OR 97420); or *Paths to Peace: A Call to Action* (contact: San Diego Unitarian Universalist Peace Network Task Force, 8220 Vincetta Dr., No. 8, La Mesa, CA 92041).

16. Write the Martin Luther King, Jr. Center for Nonviolent Social Change, 449 Auburn Ave., N.E., Atlanta, GA 30312, and obtain information about the programs they foster. Consider supporting such programs.

4: CONCILIATION / RECONCILIATION

17. Whenever possible in everyday life, abandon a formal/legalistic approach to human beings. Practice as much direct dialogue as possible, even with supposed "opponents" or "adversaries." Use negotiation, mediation, arbitration, sharing of differences.

18. Forego exclusive reliance on intermediaries such as the police and the judiciary which avoids dealing directly with people in cases of conflict. In cases of feuds and quarrels, consider using approaches such as those described in Mark Juergensmeyer's *Fighting with Gandhi,* or Roger Fisher and William Ury's *Getting to Yes; Negotiating Agreement Without Giving In.*

19. Every day, try to achieve some extent of reconciliation around you, by bringing together two or more dissenting parties — or (if you are one of the dissenting

parties) by taking steps toward reconciliation.

20. Every day, try not to antagonize at least *one* of the persons you are in touch with.

21. Try to make one new friend a week (an approach recommended by the Magic Valley Peace Project in Buhl, Idaho). This will help friendship, goodwill, and harmony grow exponentially around you.

5: SHARE IN GOVERNMENT

22. Do not consider that we have, once and for all, delegated to a few specialized individuals the task of "governing" us, and that our responsibility in participating in the process of government is thus ended. Participate in the democratic process; support a government only if it allows fair representation. Keep in touch with your elected representatives and convey your views to them — by telephone, by letter, or by personal visit. It is the basic way to make democracy work. Consult the "Tips on Letter-writing" section in *Paths to Peace: A Call To Action* (see No. 15 above.)

23. Consider practicing passive resistance to government laws that conflict with truth or the Law of Love. Consider offering sanctuary to aliens who are subjected to political repression in their country; consider practicing tax resistance, draft resistance.

24. Get involved in political activity sustained by nonviolent values. Such *focused* political effort will help make a difference in the life of our country, and help solve the current political crisis. Consider joining a political party, or participating in the creation of a new party. Encourage appropriate movements to develop greater political effectiveness.

---

25. Debureaucratize life, and as much as possible, practice decentralization. Consider these interrelated truths: *Small is beautiful; small preserves a human scale and more human relationships. Big is alienating and depersonalizing.*

26. Get involved with The Future in Our Hands, the grassroots movement for social change guided from below. The movement originated in Norway, where it has been supported by explorer Thor Heyerdahl, and has become a significant force in Scandinavian politics. It fosters recognition of a basic human solidarity, and works for a less wasteful lifestyle in the rich countries and the transfer of resources needed to abolish global poverty. Contact: The Future in Our Hands Project USA, Box 1380, Ojai, CA 93023.

27. Investigate and help disseminate specifically Gandhian approaches (practice of nonviolence, Gandhian views on regional socio-economic conversion (such as presented in a booklet by G. Ramachandra Rao). Get the statement, *Declaration of Interdependence*. For both of these, contact: The Ways of Peace and Service, P.O. Box 1315, Santa Ana, CA 92702.

28. Ponder the very considerable extent to which our country has intervened in the internal affairs of various Central American countries, and the extent to which, as a nation, we are collectively responsible for the plight of many of these countries. Consult the booklet published by the American Friends Service Committee, *The Central American War: A Guide to the U.S. Military Buildup* (obtainable from: National Action/Research on the Military Industrial Complex, AFSC, 1501 Cherry St., Philadelphia, PA 19102); or contact the Nicaragua Information Center, 2103

Woolsey St., Berkeley, CA 94705.

6: RE-EDUCATION

29. Devise alternatives to the highly competitive and intellectual-oriented approach to education which prevails in our society. Find concrete ways of fostering such alternatives, both for the education of children and young people, and the ongoing education and re-education of all of us in society.

30. Read and investigate different points of view. Learn the facts. Challenge lies with truth. Avoid mental laziness and ignorance.

31. Support the work of Educators for Social Responsibility, 23 Garden St., Cambridge, MA 02138.

32. At least two or three times a week and if possible, daily, read something by Gandhi, Albert Schweitzer, Mother Teresa, Peace Pilgrim, Dorothy Day, or similar guides (as well as analogous texts of your own tradition or denomination). Select books dealing directly with practicing service, fostering peace through the reduction of tension and conflict, or working for peace and social justice.

33. Every day, spend at least a few moments of quiet meditative time to ponder reflectively thoughts and suggestions from the above mentioned guides, and/or reflect on service and peace-oriented inspirational messages from secular or religious sources.

Consider practicing prayer and/or meditation in a sustained way. This was one of Gandhi's basic strategies. The book, *Invitation to a Great Experiment*, by Thomas E. Powers (Doubleday, 1979), contains invaluable advice and information, and includes an immensely helpful annotated bibliography. Or find a reputable teacher or guide.

34. Once or twice a month, get together with like-minded individuals who are actively exploring possibilities of selfless service. The agenda of your meetings might include: short reading of inspirational texts; perhaps a period of focusing or quiet meditative time; sharing concrete endeavors and specifics about service and work for peace; perhaps some singing; communal meal. *"Never underestimate the power of a loosely knit group working for a good cause. All of us who work for peace together, all of us who pray for peace together are a small minority, but a powerful spiritual fellowship. Our power is beyond our numbers".* (Peace Pilgrim)

35. Consider joining or forming a group or intentional community which is actively pursuing the Gandhian ideals of frugality, selfless service, and work for peace.

36. Another fundamental Gandhian strategy is fasting. How this was integrated in Gandhi's overall strategy is revealed in his *Autobiography.* Seek appropriate guidance from experienced practitioners (and your doctor). Consult *Fasting as a Way of Life,* by Alan Cott, M.D. (Bantam).

7: SHARING OF RESOURCES

37. Do not let a single day go by without practicing some form of giving. Some guidelines about giving:

Why give? Because we have received so much. Because it's not really mine; I'm just a trustee or steward. Because each one of us is part of a single family.

When to give? When asked. But give also when there is an unexpressed need.

To whom shall I give? To the one who asks. To my neighbor

with whom I have personal contact. Give to those who have basic needs.

How much to give? Give a full measure! Ten or twenty percent of what I have could be a fair amount. (Someone who gave a shivering beggar merely half of his cloak was canonized, as Saint Martin, by the Christian church.)

How to give? Lovingly. With joy and simplicity. Either as an identified giver or anonymously.

What to give? In some cases, give money, hot meals, clothes — certainly. But preferably, give the opportunity to work, give training that will enable the recipient to earn a living. Give basics: our presence, time, attention. Give peace, strength, acceptance and joy to others.

38. Practice hospitality. Open up your home. Invite people who are not likely to be invited into a home. On occasion, allow aliens, travellers, etc. to use your home as a place of rest and refreshment.

39. Investigate carefully the human needs within your own family, and your circle of friends and acquaintances, and decide what form of service or commitment you can make to some of those needs.

40. Consider the human needs within your immediate neighborhood: Those people who just moved next door, who may appreciate a few welcoming words. The family in your apartment building who can't afford a babysitter. The old lady whose eyesight is failing and who needs someone to read to her or to just sit and talk. The "latch key kids" down the block whom you could befriend. A sick person for whom you might pick up groceries. Children with academic needs, whom you could tutor.

Know your neighbor. Systematically try to engage in

conversation with neighbors *before* a crisis or acute problem develops. If you are within a so-called "unsafe neighborhood," form a team with one, two, or more like-minded individuals and together tackle the task of undertaking a neighborhood action project.

41. Endeavor to practice frugality and simplicity in a systematic and very concrete way that will cut down on waste in your life and around you. Keep in mind these truths: "Unnecessary possessions are unnecessary burdens. Many lives are cluttered not only with unnecessary possessions but also with meaningless activities" (Peace Pilgrim). For practical suggestions, contact: Alternatives, P.O Box 1707, Forest Park, GA 30051.

42. Ponder the moral responsibility we have in making investments which are morally sound in that they do not help generate more suffering or reinforce structures of injustice or exploitation in the world. For further information on socially responsible investment, write: Investor Responsibilty Research Center (IRRC), Suite 900, 1319 F Street, N.W., Washington, D.C. 20004; or Center for Economic Revitalization, Box 363, Calais Stage Road, Worcester, VT 05682.

43. Take concrete steps to help remedy malnutrition and hunger in the world. Help disseminate copies of Arthur Simon's *Bread for the World*. (Bread for the World, 6411 Chillum Place NW, Washington DC 20012), and *World Hunger: Ten Myths*, by Frances Moore Lappe and Joseph Collins (Institute for Food and Development Policy, 2588 Mission Street, San Francisco, CA 94110). To find out about ways you can get involved, write the Institute for Food and Development Policy, or The Hunger Project, 2015 Steiner

Street, San Francisco, CA 94115.

44. Develop an awareness of global overpopulation problems. Consider participating in the work of the Population Action Council, Population Institute, 110 Maryland Avenue NE, Suite 209, Washington DC 20002.

45. Participate in the work done for the alleviation of social injustice, poverty, and ecological destruction. Consider supporting the Institute for World Order, 777 United Nations Plaza, New York, NY 10017.

46. Encourage and support "natural coalitions" to address major problems, such as the Food for All program, which brings together the food industry, supermarket shoppers, and organizations working to eliminate hunger. Write: Food for All, 71 N. Center St., Redlands, CA 92373. Consider starting a Food for All program in your home town.

SUMMATION

Come to the realization that you can first change one person and that is yourself; that we should first change one country, our own. When one changes oneself it becomes possible to make changes in others; to initiate a change in our country's priorities. The Gandhian principle is one of example: inspiring others to change themselves so that eventually our institutions and government change and serve as an example to the world.

Appendices

SUGGESTED READINGS

Gandhi's Writings:

All Men Are Brothers, ed. by Krishna Kripalani. Paris: UNESCO, 1958/1972.

The Essential Gandhi: His Life, Work, and Ideas. An Anthology, ed. Louis Fischer, New York: Random House, 1962.

An Autobiography: The Story of My Experiments with Truth, Boston: Beacon Press, 1957.

Service Before Self, ed. Anand T. Hingorani. New Delhi: Gandhi Peace Foundation, 1971 (obtain from Greenleaf Books, Weare, NH 03281).

Constructive Programme: Its Meaning and Place. Ahmedabad, India: Navajivan Publ. House, 1959 (from Greenleaf Books, Weare, NH 03281).

Books About Gandhi and the Gandhian Strategy:

Beyond War: A New Way of Thinking. Palo Alto: Beyond War, 1985 (2nd edn.).

Bondurant, Joan. *Conquest of Violence: The Gandhian Philosophy of Conflict.* Berkeley: University of California Press, 1967.

Elgin, Duane. *Voluntary Simplicity: Toward a Way of Life that Is Outwardly Simple, Inwardly Rich.* New York: Wm. Morrow, 1981.

Fischer, Louis. *Gandhi: His Life and Message for the World.* New York: New American Library, 1954.

Fisher, Roger and William Ury. *Getting to Yes: Negotiating Agreement Without Giving In.* Boston: Houghton Mifflin, 1981.

Freire, Paulo. *Pedagogy of the Oppressed.* New York: Herder and Herder, 1970.

Green, Martin. *Tolstoy and Gandhi, Men of Peace: A Biography.* New York: Basic Books, 1983.

Gregg, Richard B. *The Power of Nonviolence.* New York: Schocken, 1966.

Harrison, Paul. *Inside the Third World: The Anatomy of Poverty.* New York: Viking Penguin, 1984 (2nd edn.).

Juergensmeyer, Mark. *Fighting with Gandhi: A Step-by-Step Strategy for Resolving Everyday Conflicts.* San Francisco: Harper and Row, 1984.

King, Martin Luther, Jr. *Strength to Love.* Philadelphia: Fortress Press, 1982.

Lanza del Vasto. *From Gandhi to Vinoba: The New Pilgrimage,* New York: Schocken, 1974.

Lanza del Vasto. *Principles and Precepts of the Return to the Obvious.* New York, Schocken, 1974.

Lappe, Frances Moore, and Joseph Collins. *World Hunger: Ten Myths.* San Francisco: Institute for Food and Development Policy, 1979.

Nanda, B.R. *Mahatma Gandhi: A Biography.* Woodbury, NY: Barron's, 1965.

Rawding, F.W. *Gandhi.* New York: Cambridge University Press, 1980 (A 48-page booklet with illustrations, particularly suited for young readers and school use.)

Rosenberg, Marshall B. *A Model for Nonviolent Communication.* Philadelphia: New Society Publishers, 1983.

Sale, Kirkpatrick. *Dwellers in the Land: The Bioregional Vision.* San Francisco: Sierra Club Books, 1985.

Schumacher, E.F. *A Guide for the Perplexed.* New York: Harper and Row, 1977.

Schumacher, E.F. *Small is Beautiful: Economics as if People Mattered.* New York: Harper and Row, 1973.

Schumacher, E.F. *Good Work.* New York: Harper and Row, 1979.

Sethi, J.D. *Gandhi Today.* New Delhi: Vikas Publishing House, 1979 (2nd edn.).

Sharp, Gene. *Gandhi as a Political Strategist*. Boston: Porter Sargent, 1979.

Shi, David E. *The Simple Life: Plain Living and High Thinking in American Culture*. New York: Oxford University Press, 1985.

Sider, Ron (ed.) *Living More Simply*. Downer's Grove, IL: Intervarsity Press, 1980.

Tolstoy, Leo *The Law of Violence and the Law of Love*. Santa Barbara, CA: Concord Grove Press, 1981.

Watley, William D. *Roots of Resistance: The Nonviolent Ethic of Martin Luther King, Jr.* Valley Forge, PA: Judson Press, 1985.

In this country, the best-stocked distributor of books by and about Gandhi is Greenleaf Books, Old Farm Road, Weare, New Hampshire, 03281.

A GANDHI CHRONOLOGY

October, 1869: Born at Porbandar, Kathiawad, India.

1876: Betrothed to Kasturbai (Kasturba), whom he married in 1883.

September, 1888: Sailed from Bombay to England to study law.

1891: Returned to India to practice law.

April, 1893: As lawyer for an Indian firm in Durban, South Africa, was subjected to color discrimination.

December, 1896: Settled with his family in Durban, South Africa.

1899: Organized Indian Ambulance Corps for the British in Boer War.

1901-1902: Returned with his family to India, where he traveled extensively before practicing law in Bombay.

1902-1903: Returned to South Africa at the request of the Indian community. Drafted the first petition sent by Indians to a South African government legislature. Established a weekly journal, *Indian Opinion.*

1904: Organized Phoenix settlement near Durban.

March, 1906: Organized the Indian Ambulance Corps at the time of the Zulu Rebellion.

January, 1908: Sentenced to Johannesburg jail for two months — the first of his imprisonments.

1913: Began penitential fast (one meal a day for four months) in atonement for moral lapse of members of his Phoenix settlement.

September, 1921: Resolved to wear only loincloth in devotion to homespun cotton and simplicity.

April 6, 1930: Broke India's salt law by picking up salt at the seashore as part of strategy to drive home the fact that the British monopoly and tax on salt were immoral — salt belonged to all and should be free to all.

November, 1933: Began a ten-day tour of all Indian provinces to help end untouchability.

October, 1940: Launched limited individual civil disobedience campaign against Indian participation in World War II.

August 9, 1942: Arrested with other Congress Party members and his wife Kasturbai, and interned in Aga Khan Palace near Poona.

February 22, 1944: Kasturbai died in detention, at age 74.

August 15, 1947: Fasted and prayed to combat riots as India was partitioned and gained independence.

January 30, 1948: Assassinated in his seventy-eighth year.

THE TRADITION OF NONVIOLENCE

PIONEERS (Gandhi's Precursors)

William Lloyd Garrison (1805-79), New England Non-Resistance Society, 1838

Henry David Thoreau (1817-62), Essay "Civil Disobedience" 1849

John Ruskin (1819-1900), *Unto This Last*, 1862

Leo Tolstoy (1828-1910), *The Kingdom of God is Within You*, 1893

MOHANDAS KARAMCHAND GANDHI (1869-1948)
First major public application of nonviolence, South Africa, 1907

TWENTIETH CENTURY
HIGHLIGHTS OF NONVIOLENCE

UNITED STATES

American Friends Service Committee (AFSC) founded 1917, Nobel Peace Prize, 1947

Jane Addams (1860-1935), Nobel Prize 1931; Women's International League for Peace and Freedom (WILPF) 1916

Emily G. Balch (1867-1946), Nobel Prize 1946

U.S. Fellowship of Reconciliation (FOR) founded 1917

War Resisters' League (WRL) founded 1923;
    A.J. Muste, principal leader of nonviolent movement

Dorothy Day founds *Catholic Worker* newspaper 1933

Rev. Martin Luther King, Jr. (1929-68), Civil rights boycott, Montgomery, 1956, Nobel Prize, 1964

Cesar Chavez (b. 1927), United Farm Workers action, Delano, California, 1965

Vietnam War protests, 1960s-1973

Baldemar Velasquez, Farm Labor Organizing Committee, Campbell Soup boycott, 1982

Rev. John Fife, Sanctuary Movement for Central American refugees, Tucson, 1980s

---

EUROPE

Great Britain: Fellowship of Reconciliation founded 1914; Bertrand Russell (1872-1970), Russell-Einstein Manifesto, London, 1955; Greenham Common nuclear weapons protest begins 1981

West Germany: Green Party founded 1980

France and Switzerland: Romain Rolland (1866-1944); Pierre Ceresole (1879-1944), first overseas Peace Corps 1934; Lanza del Vasto (1901-81), fast in protest of war in Algeria 1957

Italy: Danilo Dolci (b. 1924), peasant roadbuilding strike, Partinico, 1956

ASIA

India: Abdul Ghaffar Khan, the "Frontier Gandhi" from 1938; Vinoba Bhave (1895-1982), Landgift Reform Campaign 1951; J.P. Narayan (1902-79), Anti-corruption political reform, Bihar, 1974; Morarji Desai, first Ghandian Premier of India, 1977

Sri Lanka: Gandhian Movement of Ariyaratne; nonviolent economics and ecology, Senanayake, 1958

Vietnam: Thich Nhat Hanh, Buddhist monk, poet, and international peace activist

Japan: Gandhian Sarvodaya Movement; Nichidatsu Fujii, Zen monk and peace activist

Korea: Kim Young Sam, human rights fast 1983

Philippines: Corazon Aquino, President, 1986

SOUTH PACIFIC

Fiji: Rev. Charles F. Andrews, abolished indenture 1920

New Zealand: Nuclear weapons protests, from 1972

Pacific Nuclear Free Zone, 1985

AFRICA

Egypt: Anwar Sadat (assass. 1981), sought Middle East peace, Nobel 1978

Rhodesia: Zulu Chief Albert Luthuli (1898?-1967), Nobel Prize 1960

Zambia: Kenneth Kaunda, statesman favorable to nonviolence

Tanzania: Julius Nyerere, statesman favorable to nonviolence

South Africa: Bishop Desmond Tutu, nonviolent resistance to
   Apartheid, Nobel Prize 1984

SOUTH AND CENTRAL AMERICA
Brazil: Archbishop Helder Camara (b. 1909), 1st Folk Peace Prize 1974
El Salvador: Archbishop Oscar Romero (assass. 1980)
Argentina: Adolfo Perez Esquivel, Nobel Prize 1980; Alfonso
   Garcia Robles, Nobel Prize 1982

For more information on the tradition of nonviolence and Gandhi's legacy, see James W. Gould, "Gandhi's Relevance Today,"
   in *Gandhi's Significance for Today,* London: Macmillan (in press).

A DECLARATION OF INTERDEPENDENCE

A contemporary statement of Gandhian values, coordinated by Guy de Mallac, Tim Lattimer and Leslie Goldman

When in the course of human evolution, it becomes necessary for all people to unite as One People, and to build a world based upon peace, justice, and order, a decent respect to the opinions of humankind requires that we should declare the causes which impel us to such integration.

We hold these truths to be self-evident, that our planet is one interdependent and interrelated life support system. That we are all children of the same creative Spirit who have a mission to love each other with all of our hearts, minds, and souls. That the basic human rights of life, liberty, dignity, and the pursuit of self-realization cannot be separated from the responsibilities we have to respect the sacredness of all life; to serve others, to act as stewards of the planet, and to actively pursue peace and justice. That the continued buildup of armaments results from self-centered, self-righteous, and myopic attitudes is a colossal waste of resources and human potential, and has set the world in motion toward inevitable planetary self-destruction. That whenever any form of government, which derives its just powers from the consent of the governed, threatens to destroy the planet in order to achieve or preserve political, economic, or ideological ends, it is the obligation of the people to alter or abolish such morally and spiritually bankrupt governments, and to institute a new order of the ages.

We, the human beings of this generation, are at a crossroads in human history: we must choose between life and death. The decisions we make as individuals and collectively will determine the path that humanity will follow. We cannot shrink from making these decisions, for to do so is to decide to abdicate our personal responsibilities to each other and to future generations. Now is the time to discard the straightjacket of a single-minded national security system, and to think more globally. Now is the time to choose life.

We must therefore recognize that the resolution of conflict through violence is not acceptable. That there can be no personal or national security without a more global security. That our human and technological resources must be directed toward constructive, life-affirming purposes rather than toward destructive military activities. That we must transcend the illusion of separateness by recognizing that there can be unity in diversity, and the diversity is truly a strength.

We, the people of Earth, recognizing the single source of our being and our essential brother/sisterhood, solemnly declare that the nation-states of the planet are free, equal, and interdependent. That we are One Humanity living on One planet, partaking of the One life. That we view Earth as our home, and ourselves as the stewards and friends of Earth and all its offspring in every race, culture, and consciousness. That we are the caretakers of this planet for our descendants, and that ours is the generation which must begin the task of renewing the world.

We declare that a necessary first step toward such renewal is the abolition of violence, especially warfare. That each of us will sow the seeds of peace within ourselves and throughout our personal relationships. We promise to resolve conflict and to be peacemakers. Let this be our assurance and insurance against war — that each one of us asserts:

"Within me, I am fostering and making peace.
And I pledge to spread peace around me."

In order to spread peace around us, we pledge not to preoccupy ourselves with the notion of enemies. And we pledge to exemplify unconditional love and unconditional forgiveness toward our fellow human beings.

We pledge to work together and with others to build a world

beyond violence and war, a world transformed; diverse yet united.

Let everyone know from this moment our Declaration of Interdependence with our community, with our country, with all of our fellow human beings, with our planet, with our universe. For the support of this Declaration, we mutually pledge to each other our love and our lives, our fortunes and our honor.

Let every living thing know each of us as a refuge, an open portal welcoming new visions and human possibilities, a sanctuary of peace, a protector of the sacred child in everyone.

Let us be the seeds of peace, let each one of us make a positive difference. For each one of us is the Earth and the fullness thereof.

GOALS FOR CONTEMPORARY AMERICAN PERSONAL AND POLITICAL ACTION
Inspired by Gandhian Values

1. MAKE A PERSONAL COMMITMENT

Commit yourself to lead a life of creative simplicity, sharing of resources, and participate in the decisions of your community and country. Make ecologically sound choices in your living. Do your own small part to bring about positive change in the world.

2. HELP RESTORE RESPONSIVENESS AND BALANCE OF POWER IN OUR GOVERNMENT

Renew the function of Congress to be responsive to the people, as mandated by the Constitution. Call for Congress to reassert its prerogatives, countering excessive power of the Presidency. Work for campaign funding reform (as suggested by Common Cause), to diminish the power of well-heeled Political Action Committees (PACs) that represent narrow special interests.

3. NEGOTIATE A RAPID HALT TO THE ARMS RACE

Work diligently with the other nuclear powers to bring about a multilateral halt to testing, production and deployment of nuclear weapons and new weapons systems. Make certain that existing nuclear treaties are observed and respected.

4. SEEK OPTIONS TO MILITARY INTERVENTION

Pursue rational alternatives to military intervention in the affairs of other countries by the United States and other powers. Support sanctions against countries that try to force their will on weaker nations.

5. SUPPORT HUMAN RIGHTS EVERYWHERE

Require that our government cease military and economic support of regimes that practice gross injustices and violate the basic human rights of their own people (modern examples might include the governments of South Africa, Israel, El Salvador).

6. SUPPORT AND STRENGTHEN THE U.N.

Encourage active participation by our country in the activities of the United Nations, the one true world forum for settling international disputes and safeguarding human rights. Improve the efficiency and strength of the U.N. to address and help solve world problems of many kinds.

7. HELP IMPROVE THE VALUES IN YOUR OWN COMMUNITY AND COUNTRY

Think globally and act locally. Help to build an ethic in your community and America that provides for human needs: decent housing, health care, good education, useful and meaningful work, and a safe and happy environment. Nurture a society that promotes the dignity and worth of human beings, and provides opportunities for them to develop their best potentials. In essence, a decent, kind and just order of free people.

8. WORK TOWARD AN END TO BIGOTRY

Promote and nurture universal acceptance of one another as we are, and an ethic of sisterhood/brotherhood. Challenge unfair attitudes and practices based on racism, sexism, elitism, and other forms of prejudice.

9. WORK FOR GLOBAL JUSTICE AND SHARING

Encourage the richer nations to be more consciously

effective in helping poorer nations, for the benefit of all. Help poor nations develop to a point where they can help themselves, through private as well as governmental activity (Oxfam America, Peace Corps, your church). As John F. Kennedy said, "If we do not help the many who are poor, we cannot save the few who are rich."

10. GET INVOLVED IN THE NATIONAL POLITICAL PROCESS

Inform yourself about the issues, vote, and work for candidates and proposals that support the values and goals outlined here. Encourage your friends to take part in the democratic process, and thereby overcome any lingering sense of discouragement or impotence—Empower one another!

(Compiled from A Call for Responsible Government and other sources by Richard Polese.)

The Author

Guy de Mallac's primary interests are in spreading the Gandhian message while emphasizing its relevance to today's world, and in fostering peace education and education in nonviolence.

He was instrumental in founding The Ways of Peace and Service (a group geared to exploring Gandhian and related values) as well as the United Peace Network, an umbrella for peace groups in Southern California. He maintains contacts with those (in this country, in India, and elsewhere) concerned with the task of presenting the Gandhian strategy in terms relevant to today's world situations. Dr. de Mallac teaches a course on nonviolence at the University of California at Irvine, where he is professor in the School of Humanities.